OUR VOICES
SPANISH AND LATINO FIGURES OF AMERICAN HISTORY™

LORETA JANETA VELÁZQUEZ
CUBAN CONFEDERATE SOLDIER

ASH IMERY-GARCIA

rosen publishing's
rosen
central

New York

For my parents, Sandra Imery and David Garcia.
I couldn't have asked for a more loving family.

Published in 2020 by The Rosen Publishing Group, Inc.
29 East 21st Street, New York, NY 10010

First Edition

Library of Congress Cataloging-in-Publication Data

Names: Imery-Garcia, Ash, author.
Title: Loreta Janeta Velázquez : Cuban Confederate soldier / Ash Imery-Garcia.
Description: First edition. | New York : Rosen Central, 2020. | Series: Our voices : Spanish and Latino figures of American history | Audience: Grades 5–8. | Includes bibliographical references and index.
Identifiers: LCCN 2018016580 | ISBN 9781508185178 (library bound) | ISBN 9781508185161 (pbk.)
Subjects: LCSH: Velazquez, Loreta Janeta, 1842–1923—Juvenile literature. | United States—History—Civil War, 1861–1865—Participation, Female—Juvenile literature. | United States—History—Civil War, 1861–1865—Participation, Cuban—Juvenile literature. | Women soldiers—Confederate States of America—Biography—Juvenile literature. | Cubans—Confederate States of America—Biography—Juvenile literature.
Classification: LCC E628 .I45 2019 | DDC 973.7/13092 [B]—dc23
LC record available at https://lccn.loc.gov/2018016580

Manufactured in the United States of America

On the cover: This portrait depicts Loreta Janeta Velázquez, a Cuban woman who fought in several of the American Civil War's major battles and served as a spy for the Confederate army.

CONTENTS

INTRODUCTION

Loreta Janeta Velázquez was a Cuban woman who assumed the identity of a white man to join the Confederate army during the Civil War. She lived as Lieutenant Harry T. Buford and fought in several major battles during the early years of the conflict. After she was arrested multiple times on suspicion of being a woman, Velázquez turned to espionage as another way to further the Southern cause. Her resourceful nature and talent for deception made her an excellent spy for the Confederacy. She assumed multiple identities and costumes to infiltrate the North. She even acted as a double agent, spying on the Union while appearing to spy for it, and collected valuable information for the South in the process.

As a spirited individual, she sought adventure and experiences typically withheld from women. She pushed against the strict gender norms of the nineteenth century and wanted to make her own path in life. Despite numerous personal setbacks, she persisted until the very end, and spent her later years travelling and promoting Confederate ideals long after the war was over. On a failed colonizing expedition to Venezuela, she marketed her Spanish language skills and served as an interpreter for a group of ex-Confederates. At the time of her death, Velázquez had faded from the public eye and died in relative obscurity.

Her legacy endures to the present through her memoir, *The Woman in Battle*, which gives readers a rare firsthand account of a woman soldier during the Civil War. Published a decade after

Loreta Janeta Velázquez is shown here dressed as Lieutenant Harry T. Buford in battle. Velázquez disguised herself as a man in order to serve in the war as a Confederate soldier.

the conflict, the book was more than six hundred pages long and received mixed reviews from the public. Written in a candid, if somewhat sensational manner, the narrative was undeniably provocative. The book detailed her participation in battle, daring adventures as a spy, and opinions about the Civil War's causes and effects.

Her story roused interest, but critics disapproved of her motivations for becoming a soldier, flirtations with both men and women, and refusal to follow the strict gender norms of the time period. Arbiters of post–Civil War America held authority over the nation's memory of the conflict. And they were quick to point out inconsistencies in Velázquez's autobiography. Her claims were scrutinized and her reputation marred by the accusation that she was a prostitute. Velázquez was declared a fraud, a label that has stuck with her and her book for more than a hundred years.

Although there is evidence that Velázquez exaggerated her experiences, and not every detail within *The Woman in Battle* can be verified, the facts are not the most important part of her legacy. Narratives that challenge society's expectations have often been accused of being false, but they remain a part of our collective consciousness. Loreta Janeta Velázquez's unconventional life remains relevant because of the reactions it has inspired, both negative and positive, and her contribution to women's history is immeasurable. As a Cuban woman whose memory refused to be diminished by time and skepticism, her story lives on.

CHAPTER ONE

A WOMAN ON HER OWN TERMS

Loreta Janeta Velázquez was born in Havana, Cuba, on June 26, 1842. The child of a wealthy Spanish *hacendado* (landowner) and an American woman of French descent, Velázquez learned to speak both English and Spanish fluently. Her father, a native of Cartagena, Spain, had been appointed an official position in the colony of Cuba a few years before Velázquez was born.

Her childhood was both Spanish and Cuban, as she spent her early years on her father's plantation in Havana. Plantation life in nineteenth-century Cuba had a rigid class and race system that shielded well-to-do colonizers from interacting closely with the natives. In many ways, Cuba's economy was comparable to the pre-war American South. Both relied on slave labor in order to profit from the land, which created a society defined by power, oppression, and agriculture. These social and political ideas would later inform Velázquez's own beliefs as a Confederate soldier.

Velázquez's family temporarily left Cuba for central Mexico in 1844. Her father inherited a substantial amount of land in San Luis Potosí and hoped to start a new life there with his wife and children. Unfortunately, much of their estate was lost as a result of the Mexican-American War, when half of Mexico's

This young banana plantation is in Havana, Cuba. Loreta Janeta Velázquez was raised on her father's plantation in Cuba during the early years of her childhood.

land was taken by the United States. The family had financially supported Mexico in the conflict and were devastated by the loss. Velazquez's father became resentful of the United States and moved his family back to Cuba. As his favorite daughter, Velazquez was greatly affected by her father's bitterness and her family's misfortune. This mistrust of the US government and the experience of growing up in a Cuban plantation both played a role in her decision to side with the Southern states in the Civil War.

MEXICAN-AMERICAN WAR

The Mexican-American War only lasted from 1846 to 1848, but the repercussions of the conflict were considerable. The United States set its sights on Mexican land in its quest to expand across North America. And after the annexation of Texas in 1845, tension between the two countries peaked.

While Mexico acknowledged that Texas was now a part of the United States, the boundary between Mexico and

This map of Mexico shows the new boundaries established after the Treaty of Guadalupe Hidalgo was signed on February 2, 1848.

(continued on the next page)

(continued from the previous page)

Texas was under contention. Mexico said that the Nueces River separated the two countries, while the United States claimed it was the Rio Grande. The dispute between the two boundaries translated into an argument over how much land the United States could acquire. After Mexico rejected an offer to sell the disputed territory, the United States set up camp past the Nueces River in a deliberate act of aggression. When Mexican forces retaliated, the United States declared war on the basis that Mexico had invaded a US territory.

After Mexico's capitol was captured by American soldiers, the Treaty of Guadalupe Hidalgo was signed in 1848 and Mexico forfeited half of its land to the United States. The land lost included not only the disputed territory of Texas, but also present-day Arizona, New Mexico, Nevada, California, Utah, and Colorado.

EDUCATION IN NEW ORLEANS

Velázquez's parents wanted a traditional future for their children and expected their daughter to marry a respectable Spanish gentleman. During the nineteenth century, it was not uncommon for Cuban families to send their daughters abroad to learn English and the domestic arts necessary to be considered for marriage. In 1849, Velázquez's family sent her to New Orleans to receive an education.

The United States was a very different cultural experience for young Velázquez. During the Mexican-American War, Mexicans had been painted as simple-minded savages and that racism spread to affect most Latinos and Hispanics living in the United States. Velázquez came from a privileged background in Cuba, where her family was a part of the ruling social class, and this kind of racial discrimination against someone of her status must have shocked her. Velázquez thought of herself as equal to white Southerners, even if most Americans would have argued otherwise.

As an old-world port, New Orleans was a melting pot of different ethnicities and races. While the city was a key player in the South's economy and home to the nation's leading slave market, it also had the largest and wealthiest population of free people of color. To be "white" in New Orleans meant that someone was a paler person of a racially mixed background with enough money to secure themselves above certain types of discrimination. There were more opportunities for racial passing, or when a person of color is accepted as white, in New Orleans than there were in most of the United States. Velázquez learned to emphasize her heritage as a way distinguish herself as a person of privilege. Because race worked on a spectrum and was not a fixed identity, individuals had to intentionally cultivate a sense of place and belonging. In her memoir, Velázquez frequently refers to herself as a "Spanish" woman and focused on her colonial roots as an important class and racial marker.

GIRLHOOD HEROINES

Despite pressures to assimilate, young Velázquez was a passionate girl with unusual interests. In her studies, she learned about Joan of Arc, a young woman who donned armor and led the French to victory in the Hundred Years' War in the fifteenth

Catalina de Erauso was known as La Monja Alférez, or the Nun Lieutenant, after she left the convent and disguised herself as a man to become a soldier.

century. Velázquez was enamored by Joan of Arc's story and grew up with a desire to emulate her deeds of valor. Velázquez writes that Joan of Arc is an example of "what a woman may do if she only dares, and dares to do greatly." She was fascinated by women warriors and her girlhood heroines included daring figures such as Catalina De Erauso, who left convent life to become a soldier, and Apolonia Jagiello, a Polish revolutionary who flouted feminine conventions. Drawn to these powerful women, Velázquez spent her childhood wishing for an opportunity to fight in the name of a cause larger than herself.

MARRIAGE

When Velázquez became a teenager, her parents wanted her leave behind her girlish aspirations and accept more conventional pursuits. Her family had arranged for their daughter to marry a Spaniard she called "Raphael R." (Velázquez frequently omitted last names in her autobiography, likely as a way to protect their privacy). However, Velázquez rebelled against traditional Spanish customs and her parents' wishes. She fell in love with the boyfriend of her best friend, a young American army officer named "William," and the pair soon married.

Barely more than a girl herself, Velázquez had three children with William by the age of nineteen. Two of them died from illness and the other passed away shortly after birth. In the course of her marriage to a Southern-born soldier, Velázquez had transitioned from a schoolgirl to a young woman. She had become more American in thought and manner and her marriage helped ground her in Southern life.

CIVIL WAR BEGINS

When the Civil War started in 1861, President Abraham Lincoln had just been elected to lead the nation without a single Southern electoral vote. Lincoln had run on a platform that supported banning slavery in all US territories. The Southern states believed this was a violation of their constitutional rights and a part of larger plan to abolish slavery completely. The South, which Velázquez called home, felt disenfranchised. Before Lincoln's inauguration, the Southern states began to secede. When William's home state of Texas decided to leave the Union, he resigned his position in the US Army

Abraham Lincoln was elected the sixteenth president of the United States in 1861, without support from many of the Southern states.

and joined the Confederates. Many young men in New Orleans, whether they owned slaves or not, also volunteered to fight for the South as a point of pride and a desire to retain their way of life.

CHAPTER TWO

A WOMAN IN MALE COSTUME IS A MAN

W hen William was appointed to train Confederate recruits in Florida, Velázquez wanted to join him as an equal. She proposed that she dress as a man in order to enlist with the Southern troops, but her husband attempted to dissuade her. He believed camp life would be too vulgar and dangerous for a woman, and asked that she stay in New Orleans. At this point in her life, her children had died and William was all that Velázquez had left to tie her to domesticity. Over the course of her marriage to an American soldier, her interest in military life had grown and she fully sympathized with the newly formed Confederacy.

A SOLDIER'S DISGUISE

Velázquez was committed to joining the fight. Against her husband's wishes, she went to a trusted tailor who "understood how to mind his own business by not bothering himself too much about other people's affairs," and asked him to make half a dozen fine wire net shields which she wore over her chest. She explains that they were very satisfactory in concealing her true form and, "in giving me something of the shape of a man." Over the wire shield, she also wore a fitted silk shirt, a shoulder brace, and a heavy belt which she used to "make the waistband of my pantaloons stand out to the proper number of inches." Velázquez concluded that any woman with the proper undergarments and confidence could pass as a man, even to the closest of observers.

After she acquired a complete military outfit, she spent some time settling into her new persona and carefully practiced a masculine manner. Velázquez completed her disguise by

While disguised as a man, Velázquez could participate in the war and had access to freedoms that were unavailable to her as a woman.

CIVIL WAR CAUSES

The American Civil War lasted from 1861 to 1865 between the Northern and Southern states. The conflict began shortly after the presidential election of 1860, when longstanding controversy over the legal status of slavery reached a tipping point. While the northern half of the United States had gradually outlawed slavery as industrialization spread, the Southern states remained an agricultural plantation society that relied heavily on slave labor.

After President Abraham Lincoln won the election in 1860, without even being on the ballot in ten Southern states, many Southern leaders felt that they were no longer being represented by the federal government. Lincoln's victory triggered the secession of eleven states in the American South, who banded together to form the Confederate States of America.

The Confederacy, or the South, argued that it was within the rights of the states to leave the Union and that the federal government shouldn't be allowed to dictate the laws of the individual states, such as the abolition of slavery. They feared that the Union was on the path to abolishing slavery altogether, and that they no longer had an avenue to promote their pro-slavery policies. While there were varied opinions regarding slavery in the Union states, most individuals were indifferent on the subject as large-scale manufacturing and cheap immigrant labor had eradicated the need for slaves in the North. Alternatively, the Confederate states believed they were fighting for the preservation of the Southern way of life and that emancipation would destroy their economy.

cutting her hair and donning a false mustache. She went on a few exploratory trips in public as a man and hid any traces of femininity from her person. After some preparation, she moved on to her primary goal of recruiting as many men to the Confederate army as possible, so that she could meet her husband in Florida. Velázquez believed that William would be so impressed when he saw that she had outfitted an entire battalion, that he couldn't possibly remain upset that she had gone against his wishes. And while she hoped that William would be proud of her efforts, she also resolved that if she could not serve with him, she would participate in the war with or without his assistance.

WIDOWED

Velázquez succeeded in recruiting thirty-six men and marched them to Pensacola, Florida, to begin military training. William was genuinely surprised by her arrival, and after Velázquez pulled him aside privately to discuss the issue of her attire, he acquiesced that his wife was fit to be a soldier. Velázquez writes that upon "seeing the uselessness of further argument," William, "took command of the men and commenced putting them in training." The moment was a victory for Velázquez and she was proud of what she accomplished.

Unfortunately, soon after Velázquez and her husband reached an agreement to work alongside each other in the war, William was killed during a training exercise. As he attempted to show the new recruits the proper way to use a rifle, the weapon backfired and he died. Velázquez had the opportunity to leave the army and live life as a widow. Instead, she channeled her grief into military action and chose to commit to her new identity as a Confederate soldier.

LIVING AS LIEUTENANT HARRY T. BUFORD

During the Civil War, the strict social constructions of gender, class, and to some extent, race, were shaken up just enough that some individuals found ways to transcend barriers. Women from all backgrounds moved from the private sphere of the home and childrearing into the public eye. They wanted to join the war effort, whether that meant assisting from the sidelines or fighting on the battlefield. It's estimated that hundreds of women dressed as men to become soldiers, many of whom traveled with their husbands or male family members.

Without the trappings of her old life, Velázquez was free to undergo a complete transformation and begin living as a man full-time. Operating under the name Lieutenant Harry T. Buford, she left her recruits in Florida and set off on her own—hoping to have more freedom as an unaffiliated soldier. While it may seem unlikely that Velázquez was not immediately discovered

WOMEN'S ROLES IN THE CIVIL WAR

Civil War academics have traditionally centered history around the work done by men in the battlefield and the political arena. Few scholars have discussed the contributions that women made during the war, and even then, women are often pushed to the margins, discussed only in terms of what they did to support the patriarchal systems which oppressed them.

In reality, women from all racial, class, and ethnic backgrounds were an essential part of the action. While much of the literature about Civil War women emphasizes their participation as nurturers—women who donated food, seamstresses who made uniforms for soldiers, or fundraisers who rallied support for the cause—there were many women who stepped outside of traditional roles to fight for their beliefs. Women sympathetic of union and disunion alike worked as nurses on the battlefield, served as spies and soldiers, and engaged in political debate. Women, particularly black women, worked to establish refugee camps for former slaves who had escaped to the North and were some of the many unsung heroes of the era.

Mary Tippee was a French woman who served with the Union army. Tippee sold goods to soldiers, traveled with them into battle, and worked in the regimental hospital.

to be a woman, the strict societal expectations of the nineteenth century acted in her favor. Standards of behavior for both genders were oppressively rigid, and it wouldn't have occurred to most onlookers that someone acting in a masculine manner and wearing pants could be a woman. The United States was in the middle of a national crisis and medical inspections required to join the army were significantly relaxed. If any man (or woman) wished to enlist, they needed to do little more than show up and report for duty. In addition, the Union and Confederate troops were some of the youngest in

This photograph shows the Home Guard White Mountain Rangers. Home Guards were volunteers who protected the home front during the Civil War and were considered an informal last line of defense.

US history. The conflict attracted many volunteers, and it wasn't unusual for young boys to enlist. Soldiers without facial hair or whose voices had yet to drop to the tenor of an adult man were common. Velázquez could have easily passed as a boyish soldier with a higher-pitched voice. All of these factors played a significant role in Velázquez's ability to hide in plain sight.

FREEDOM AND INDEPENDENCE

Velázquez writes that while many soldiers commented on her petite figure and jaunty air, she was determined to hold her own on the battlefield and believed she was, "as good a man as any of them." As a soldier, Velázquez had access to experiences that would have been forbidden to her as a woman. She could travel independently, achieve more economic equality, and express her opinions freely without the confining social conventions of womanhood.

It's easy to assume that women soldiers in the Civil War fought for the same reason as men. Certainly patriotism, adventure, and ideological beliefs played a critical role in their decision, but it's also important to realize that women who passed as men during the conflict were able to live with more freedom and independence that they could have otherwise. After having experienced the liberties of being a soldier, Velázquez writes, "I have no hesitation in saying that I wish I had been created a man instead of a woman."

CHAPTER THREE

FIGHTING FOR THE SOUTHERN CAUSE

Although Velázquez wanted to support the Confederate cause any way necessary, she was eager to engage in real warfare, and informally attached herself to the regiment commanded by General Bernard E. Bee. As General Bee's men marched towards combat north of Manassas, Virginia, Velázquez joined them before they reached Bull Run creek. Velázquez had participated in smaller skirmishes with other brigades, but she was intent on maintaining her independence, even in war, where it is often necessary to fall in line with the larger order. Velázquez wrote that being an independent soldier enabled her to choose her own position in battle, and that she had a "better opportunity of distinguishing (herself)" without the binding ties of a particular troop. This desire for freedom would impact her performance as a soldier throughout her military career, to both her benefit and detriment, as it allowed her to be closer to the action, but prevented her from forming strong ties with her countrymen.

THE BATTLE OF BULL RUN

On the morning of July 21, 1861, before the Battle of Bull Run, Velázquez says that she felt, "The supreme moment of my life had arrived, and all the glorious aspirations of my romantic

The Battle of Bull Run was fought on July 21, 1861. It was the first major battle of the Civil War and Velázquez's first experience in serious combat.

girlhood were on the point of realization." She readied herself for combat and was positioned in the center of the battle, where the Union initiated a surprise attack. Southern troops were at an initial disadvantage, and as the fight continued throughout the morning, they were forced to pull back as more Northern soldiers crossed Bull Run.

Later that afternoon, Confederate reinforcements arrived from Shenandoah Valley, among them a group of Virginians under the direction of a then unknown general named Thomas J. Jackson. General Jackson was able to construct a defensive line of around six hundred men backed by artillery along Henry House Hill. In Velázquez's account of the battle, she writes that Bee rallied his men with a cry of "Victory or death! See how Jackson stands there like a stone wall." The troops shouted back the phrase and mustered behind it. Their chant became General "Stonewall" Jackson's nickname, which he and his brigade famously carried for the rest of the war. Additional Southern reinforcements broke the Union flank and Jackson's troops held their ground.

Velázquez fought alongside her companions with fervor, and while both sides suffered severe casualties, her enthusiasm for battle was strengthened by the South's success. As the first major encounter of the Civil War, the Battle of Bull Run was an important victory that emboldened the Confederate cause and reinforced Velázquez's decision to fight for the Southern army.

General "Stonewall" Jackson is shown here with his troops at the Battle of Bull Run. Jackson gained the respect of Union and Confederate military leaders and was considered a Southern war hero.

THE BATTLE OF BALL'S BLUFF

Just three months later, Velázquez was back on the battlefield. The

Battle of Ball's Bluff, while a smaller conflict, had major political implications that would affect the rest of the war. On the evening of October 20, 1861, the Union army sent a scouting party across the Potomac River to find the location of the Confederate troops. In the darkness of night, an inexperienced Union leader mistook a line of trees for an unguarded Confederate camp. His misinformation led to troops attacking the "camp" early the next day. After realizing that there wasn't a camp at all, the Union army encountered a company from the Mississippi Infantry and a fight began.

Colonel Edward Baker, a US senator, attempted to reinforce the Union soldiers, but with only a handful of small boats available to transport troops, the process was slow and lasted throughout the day. Meanwhile, the Confederates were able to drive many of the Northern soldiers over the bluff and into the Potomac River. Many men drowned and more surrendered. When Colonel Baker was killed, the Union resistance was defeated. On describing these early Confederate victories, Velázquez writes, "I would not have missed it for the wealth of the world, and was more than repaid for all that I had undergone, and all the risks to my person and my womanly reputation that I incurred, in being not only a spectator, but an actor in such a sublime, living drama."

SLAVE OWNERSHIP

As a Cuban woman searching for a sense of identity in the United States, Velázquez fought for a cause that did not consider her best interests, although she certainly believed otherwise. The Civil War was first and foremost a conflict about the institution of slavery, and while Velázquez was a marginalized individual, she was nonetheless complicit in the oppression of others and supportive of slavery's survival.

Velázquez purchased a black man named "Bob" with whom she traveled throughout most of the war. Bob was a comrade in arms, and while it's not known whether he fought purely under Velázquez's orders, it was atypical for slaves to carry weapons in the Confederate army. In fact, women and black men were forbidden from participating in the war as combatants and both groups did not have full citizenship rights. As a Hispanic woman, slave ownership may have shielded her from certain types of scrutiny and bolstered the lie that Velázquez was a white Confederate man. Her decision to treat another human being as property was undeniably heinous and should not be excused. However, it's important to understand the ways in which systemic racism affects everyone's choices not just those most privileged or oppressed.

If anyone knew of Lieutenant Buford's hidden identity, it would have been Bob. Velázquez traveled with her slave from battle to battle and it's likely he was privy to her secret. After the Battle of Shiloh, Bob and Velázquez were separated and Velázquez believed that he went to the North, where he could live as a free man. After a half-hearted inquiry, she chose not to pursue him.

DONELSON

By the time Velázquez reached Fort Donelson, she had become a seasoned veteran. Her earlier enthusiasm for battle began to fade and the realities of the conflict weighed heavily on her mind. On February 13, 1862, the Union army surrounded Fort Donelson and initiated several small attacks to probe the fort's

BLACK SOLDIERS IN THE CIVIL WAR

The Union and the Confederacy were reluctant to arm black soldiers, and it was only after two years into the war that black men were legally allowed to enlist. Military commanders on both sides of the conflict viewed black men as a liability, and were uncertain whether black troops would shoot at their white comrades, the enemy, or simply run away.

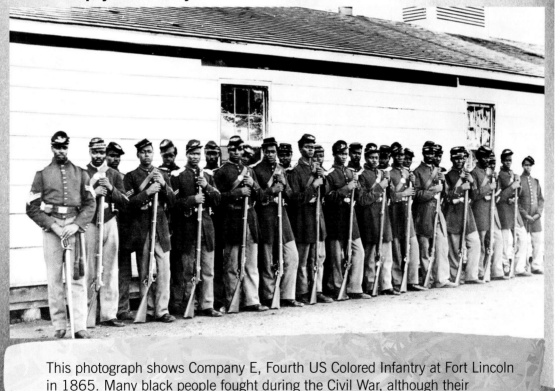

This photograph shows Company E, Fourth US Colored Infantry at Fort Lincoln in 1865. Many black people fought during the Civil War, although their participation has historically been overlooked.

(continued on the next page)

(continued from the previous page)

While motivations are difficult to determine, it's likely that many black people viewed participation in the Civil War as a path to citizenship and greater liberties. Military service was seen as an avenue toward freedom for black men, even if that was not a legal reality, and they clamored to enlist in the hope that it would lead to a better life. In particular, many black Union soldiers were proud to fight for emancipation, although the abolitionist mindset was actively discouraged by white Union leaders. Meanwhile, black confederates were either slaves in combat or free men who served in all-black units.

Historically, many oppressed people have risked their lives on the battlefield in order to achieve freedoms that would not otherwise be possible. While it's rare that soldiers maintain those freedoms after the conflict is over, when oppressed and oppressor fight alongside as equals, it becomes more difficult to deny another human being their rights.

defenses. Two days later, Confederates retaliated and attempted a surprise counterattack. Unfortunately for the South, Northern troops outnumbered the Southern soldiers and they were able to capture the fort. The Confederates eventually surrendered the garrison to the Union on February 16, 1862.

It was the first battle that Velázquez engaged in where the Confederates lost, and the defeat was painful. In many ways, the loss of Fort Donelson was the beginning of the end in Velázquez's eyes. She describes the aftermath in gruesome detail, noting that the bodies of her fallen comrades were "heaped together, six or seven feet high" and that the air was filled with the groans of the wounded, some of whom, "besought the surgeons to kill them and end their misery." After witnessing the horrors of combat, she no longer felt confident that the South would win the war.

SHILOH

Two months later, when the Battle of Shiloh took place on April 6, 1862, Velázquez was unaware that it would be her final battle as Lieutenant Buford. Disenchanted and demoralized by the South's defeat at Donelson, Velázquez rallied for another fight, but her hopes for a swift end to the war and a Confederate victory were dashed.

There were considerable casualties at the Battle of Shiloh on April 6, 1862. Both sides of the conflict recognized that the Civil War would be longer and more difficult than anticipated.

Although the fighting lasted only two days, it resulted in more than twenty-three thousand casualties, making it the bloodiest battle in American history at the time. The South made some initial gains, but the North's counterattack forced Confederate forces to retreat from the area, ending their hopes of blocking the Union's advance. Velázquez wrote, "To be a second Joan of Arc was a mere girlish fancy," which her, "experiences as a soldier had dissipated forever." She would never strike another blow for the Confederacy as a soldier.

CHAPTER FOUR

DISILLUSIONMENT WITH THE WAR

As Velázquez helped bury the dead after the Battle of Shiloh, she was injured in the arm and shoulder by an exploding shrapnel shell. Seriously wounded, she sought medical treatment, but her injury cost her dearly. An Army doctor discovered that she was a woman. With her disguise revealed, it was difficult for Velázquez to continue living as Lieutenant Buford. Faced with serious repercussions, such as jail time and potentially being convicted of treason, Velázquez sought new prospects in New Orleans as a woman.

BECOMING A SPY

New Orleans had been overtaken by Union troops and the city was rampant with fear as well as opportunity for intrepid individuals comfortable with dangerous work. Velázquez began a new career acting as a spy for the Confederates and used her reclaimed feminine dress to obtain information from Union soldiers who had set up blockades around the city.

After collecting useful information from the enemy, Velázquez gained a reputation as a valuable spy and was given more prestigious assignments by the Confederate Secret Service.

This portrait depicts Pauline Cushman, an actress who became a spy for the Union army during the Civil War. President Lincoln awarded her the honorary title of major for her service.

Under orders from the Southern army, she spent a great deal of time traveling to the North under different aliases. She adopted a multitude of male and female disguises in order to cross enemy lines: pretending to be a mistreated Southern woman defecting to the North, an English widow stuck in the United States, a Union sympathizer, and other assumed identities.

Velázquez felt well-suited for espionage, as she had spent years keeping her own secrets on the battlefield. She believed that being a woman gave her a distinct advantage as a spy, as most people assumed that a respectable lady would never go into her line of work. Velázquez writes, that for "an enterprise that requires real finesse, a woman will be likely to accomplish far more than a man."

Her primary responsibilities involved gathering information from the Union about potential military developments, passing along secret messages to the allies in the North, and smuggling money and goods. Although this last task encompassed much of her time in the Secret Service, Velázquez was conflicted by the implications of how much capital changed hands. While she enjoyed the work, she began to believe the conflict was motivated more by greed than by ideological differences, and became further disillusioned with the war.

Velázquez was conscripted to work under the esteemed Northern Colonel Lafayette C. Baker. As a double agent, she gave the appearance of spying for the North, while in actuality, she obtained Union intelligence for the Confederacy. This was a remarkable accomplishment, as it required her to juggle many secrets and identities at once. However, as the Civil War reached its conclusion, Velázquez lost her sense of direction. She had labored for the Confederacy for years without much hope that they would win the war. As both a Northern and Southern agent, it became clear that her loyalties lay with more with herself rather than a particular side in the conflict.

After the war ended and President Lincoln was assassinated, Colonel Baker tasked her with finding a female Confederate spy who had infiltrated the North. Velázquez immediately understood that the woman she was supposed to search for was herself, and that if discovered, she would be implicated in the assassination plot and hung as a traitor.

TRAVELS AFTER THE WAR

Velázquez decided that it was no longer prudent for her to continue acting as a spy. While she maintained that she was loyal to the Confederate cause, her time in the North had erased some of her prejudices against its people and the federal government. She believed that in time both the North and South would "be able to raise the nation to a pitch of greatness."

Satisfied with her career as a soldier and spy, Velázquez left the United States and traveled through Europe with her brother and visited parts of South America. She went on a failed emigration trip to Venezuela with a group of ex-Confederates, but was forced to leave after they were accused of attempting to colonize the country. Back in the US, she traveled west to join the gold rush, but was too late to be successful. She was married and widowed multiple times, and gave birth to a son whom she raised primarily on her own. Suffering from money troubles, Velázquez wrote her experiences in the form of a memoir, which she hoped would provide her with enough income to care for herself and her child.

General Jubal Early's writing shaped the South's identity after the Civil War. He framed the Confederacy's defeat as an honorable struggle and was critical of ideas that challenged his own.

RECEPTION OF WOMAN IN BATTLE

After Velázquez's autobiography was published in 1876, the book received substantial criticism. Social commentators scrutinized her story and found the details to be sensational and tawdry. Confederate General Jubal Early, one of the respected arbiters of truth on the Civil War, read Velázquez's account and declared it fiction. Velázquez wrote about the conflict and the Confederate troops without reservation and many felt threatened by her candor.

As a Cuban woman, Velázquez was incredibly dangerous to the creation of a Confederate Civil War legacy. To men like Early, who took it upon themselves to judge and curate the outcomes of the war, Velázquez's very identity challenged the status quo. Rumors that she was a fraud and a prostitute gained traction. She was referred to as "camp follower," a term which meant a woman who had sex with soldiers for money. Marginalized by both her race and gender, Velázquez was an easy target to discredit. The public didn't know what to make of her story and she was accused of being a woman of loose morals. Her book was labeled as a hoax and

SARAH EMMA EDMONDS

Sarah Emma Edmonds was a Union soldier and spy. She was the only other woman besides Velázquez to write about her experiences as a female combatant during the Civil War, and her memoir became a national bestseller when it was published in 1864. Edmonds was born in Canada, but dressed as a man to cross into the United States independently. Edmonds felt that it was her duty to serve her new country, and she maintained her disguise so she could enlist in the Union army. She fought in several major battles under the name Franklin Thompson. She also

Sarah Emma Edmonds was a Union spy, soldier, and nurse. She and Velázquez both wrote memoirs about their war experiences, but their work was received differently by critics.

worked as a spy, a male field nurse, and pursued interests unusual for women at the time. Her book, *Nurse and Spy in the Union army*, was an outstanding success and Edmonds became a popular figure.

The differences between Edmonds and Velázquez are minor, but the details of their narratives greatly affected how the public received their autobiographies. While Edmonds disguised herself as a man because

(continued on the next page)

(continued from the previous page)

she wanted to help others, Velázquez openly stated that she joined the Confederates because she sought adventure. Edmonds' donated the profits from her book to help wounded soldiers, while Velázquez wrote her autobiography as way to earn money for herself and her son. And when Edmonds took on the traditional role of wife and mother after the war, Velázquez continued to live an unconventional life.

Velázquez was pushed into obscurity. Effectively erased from the history books, her story has carried the stigma of inauthenticity for more than a century.

LEGACY

Velázquez exists in the public record until 1902, although it is not known exactly when she died. Her book remains in print and *The Woman in Battle* continues to provoke debate, admiration, and incredulity. Her narrative has shaped how we view women during the Civil War and her contributions to history are immeasurable. She pushed against social norms and lived life on her own terms. Loreta Janeta Velázquez is a testament to what women can accomplish despite society's expectations.

1842 Loreta Janeta Velázquez is born in Havana, Cuba.

1844 Velázquez's father inherits land in San Lois Potosí. The Velázquez family moves to Mexico to start a new life.

1846–48 The Mexican American War only lasts two years, but when it ends, Mexico concedes half of its land to the United States. The Velázquez family lost much of their estate after the war.

1849 Velázquez's family sends her to New Orleans, Louisiana to complete her education and prepare her for marriage.

1856 Velázquez rebels against her parents' wishes and secretly marries an American soldier.

November 6, 1860 Abraham Lincoln is elected President of the United States without a single Southern electoral vote. Many Southern states feel that they are no longer represented by the federal government.

April 12, 1861 The American Civil War begins. The Southern states begin to secede from the Union to form the Confederacy.

July 21, 1861 The First Battle of Bull Run takes place just north of Manassas, Virginia. The Confederates are victorious and Velázquez is able to participate in battle for the first time.

October 21, 1861 The Battle of Ball's Bluff takes place is Loudoun County, Virginia. After mistaking a line of trees for Confederate tents, Union forces suffer a humiliating defeat.

February 12–16, 1862 The Battle of Fort Donelson takes place near the Tennessee-Kentucky border. The Northern army wins, which ensures that Kentucky will stay in the Union, giving them a significant tactical advantage over the Confederates.

April 6–7, 1862 The Battle of Shiloh takes place in Hardin County, Tennessee. The Confederates lose and there were significant casualties on both sides.

1862 Velázquez retires as a soldier and becomes a spy for the Confederates.

1865 The Civil War ends after the Union defeats the South. The Confederate States collapse, slavery is abolished, and the Southern states are absorbed back into the Union.

1876 Velázquez's memoir, *The Woman in Battle*, appears in print to mixed reviews. Velázquez is accused of being a fraud and a prostitute.

1902 Velázquez disappears from the public record. It is not known exactly when she died.

GLOSSARY

abolitionist Someone who fought for the legal end of slavery, particularly the enslavement of blacks in the United States.

annexation When a territory becomes a part of a country, such as when Texas became a part of the United States.

arbiter An individual who has authority over what the public deems important.

disenfranchise To remove power from another.

double agent An individual who pretends to be spy for a government or agency, when they are actually spying on that government or agency.

electoral vote Votes cast by the representatives of each state that determine who will be the next president of the United States.

emancipation Liberation, particularly for enslaved blacks in the United States.

espionage The act of spying or being a spy, generally to obtain military or political information from a particular government.

ethnicity Someone's cultural or regional identity.

gender Being male or female, as perceived by the society or culture in which one exists.

gender roles Learned behaviors that are considered acceptable and appropriate for one's perceived gender.

ideology A collection of ideas or beliefs that informs one's actions.

industrialization The process by which human labor is made more efficient through mechanization or mechanical advancements.

liability A negative asset, a person or behavior that is seen as disadvantageous.

marginalize To place an individual or a group in position of less power and importance, to relegate them to place outside of the dominant culture.

patriarchy A society in which men have more power and women are prevented from obtaining power of their own.

race Physical attributes such as skin color that are used to characterize and group individuals together.

secede To formally break away from a larger union, such as when the Southern states left the larger federal government.

status quo The way things are at the present time, especially as related to social or political matters.

systemic racism Racism that permeates society through its laws, structures, and norms.

FOR MORE INFORMATION

Chicana/Latina Foundation (CLF)

1419 Burlingame Ave. Suite W2
Burlingame, CA 94010
(650) 373-1083
Website: http://www
.chicanalatina.org
Facebook:
@ChicanaLatinaFoundation
YouTube: Chicana Latina
Foundation
The Chicana Latina Foundation
seeks to empower Latinas
in higher education and
the workplace. They
provide scholarships for
Latinas, mentorship, skill
building workshops, and a
community for future and
present Latina leaders.

Civil War Trust

Civil War Trust Corporate Office
1156 15th Street NW, Suite 900
Washington, DC 20005
(202) 367-1861
Website: http://www.civilwar
.org
Facebook, Twitter, and
Instagram: @civilwartrust
YouTube: Civil War Trust

The Civil War Trust is a
nonprofit organization
dedicated to preserving
famous American Civil War
battlegrounds. They also
seek to inform the public of
the important history and
value in these spaces.

Daughters of Union Veterans of the Civil War

National Headquarters and
Museum
503 South Walnut Street
Springfield, IL 62705
(217) 544-0616
Website: http://www.duvcw.org
Facebook: @DUVCfans
The Daughters of Union
Veterans of the Civil War
is an organization for the
lineal descendants of Union
Civil War Veterans. They
encourage the public to
remember the important
roles that women played
during the Civil War era and
honor the memory of Union
soldiers.

Grand Army of the Republic Museum and Library

4278 Griscom Street
Philadelphia, PA 19124
(215) 289-6484
Website: http://www.garmuslib
.org
Facebook: @GrandArmyOfThe
RepublicMuseumAnd
Library
The Grand Army of the
Republic is committed to
preserving artifacts from
the American Civil War and
to keeping the memory of
those who served in the
conflict alive.

Jubal A. Early Preservation Trust

PO Box 638
Rocky Mount, VA 24151
Website: http://www.jubalearly
.org
Facebook: @jubalearly.org
The Jubal A. Early
Preservation Trust is
dedicated to preserving
the accomplishments of
Confederate General Jubal
A. Early. The Trust maintains
Early's childhood home

place, which has been
carefully restored and is
open to the public.

Preserve Louisiana Old Governor's Mansion

502 North Boulevard
Baton Rouge, LA 70802
(225) 343-2464
Website: http://www
.preserve-louisiana.org
Facebook: @PreserveLouisiana
Preserve Louisiana (formerly
the Foundation for Historical
Louisiana) was formed
to preserve Louisiana's
famous historical sites and
to educate the public about
the state's history.

Victorian Society in America

1636 Sansom Street
Philadelphia, PA 19103
(215) 636-9873
Website: http://www
.victoriansociety.org
Facebook, Twitter, and
Instagram: @VicSocAmerica

FOR FURTHER READING

Alberti, Enigma, and Tony Cliff. *Mary Bowser and the Civil War Spy Ring*. New York, NY: Workman Publishing, 2016.

Baptiste, Tracey. *The Civil War and Reconstruction Era*. New York, NY: Britannica Educational Publishing in Association with Rosen Educational Services, 2016.

Baumann, Susan. *Black Civil War Soldiers: The 54th Massachusetts Regiment*. New York, NY: Rosen Publishing, 2014.

Chang, Ina. *A Separate Battle: Women and the Civil War*. New York, NY: Puffin Books, 1996.

Crane, Stephen. *The Red Badge of Courage (Annotated) An Episode of the American Civil War*. San Francisco, CA: Plympton, 2016. Ebook.

Ford, Carin T. *Women in the Civil War Through Primary Sources*. Berkeley Heights, NJ: Enslow Publishers, 2013.

Jones, Viola, and Philip Wolny. *A Primary Source Investigation of the Underground Railroad*. New York, NY: Rosen Publishing, 2016.

Loria, Laura. *The Mexican-American War*. New York, NY: Rosen Publishing, 2018.

Otfinkoski, Steven. *The Civil War* (Step Into History). New York, NY: Scholastic, 2017.

Ziff, Marsha. *The Reconstruction of the South After the Civil War in United States History*. Berkeley Heights, NJ: Enslow Publishers, 2014.

BIBLIOGRAPHY

Alemán, Jesse. "Crossing the Mason-Dixon Line in Drag: The Narrative of Loreta Janeta Velasquez, Cuban Woman and Confederate Soldier." In *Look Away! The U.S. South in New World Studies*, edited by Jon Smith and Deborah Cohn, 110–29. Durham, NC: Duke University Press, 1994.

Bergeron, Arthur W., and Richard M. Rollins. *Black Southerners in Gray: Essays on Afro-Americans in Confederate Armies*. Redondo Beach, CA: Rank and File Publications, 1994.

Carter, María Agui. Rebel: *Loreta Velazquez, Secret Soldier of the American Civil War*. Documentary. United States: Public Broadcast Service. 2013.

Davis, William C. *Inventing Loreta Velazquez: Confederate soldier impersonator, media celebrity, and con artist*. Carbondale, IL: Southern Illinois University Press, 2016.

Dowie, Ménie Muriel. *Women Adventurers*. London, UK: T. F. Unwin, 1893. Nineteenth Century Collections Online. Retrieved February 27, 2018. http://tinyurl.galegroup.com/tinyurl/5zd6v0.

Eggleston, Larry G. *Women in the Civil War: Extraordinary Stories of Soldiers, Spies, Nurses, Doctors, Crusaders, and Others*. Jefferson, NC: McFarland, 2003.

Hargrove, Hondon B. *Black Union Soldiers in the Civil War*. Jefferson, NC: McFarland, 2003.

Lossing, Benson J. *A History of the Civil War 1861–65: And the Causes that Led Up to the Great Conflict*. New York, NY: The War Memorial Association, 1912.

Massey, Mary Elizabeth. *Women in the Civil War*. Lincoln, NB: University of Nebraska Press, 1994.

McArthur, Jeff. *The Forgotten Grave: Women Soldiers of the American Civil War*. Documentary. United States: Jeff McArthur. 2007.

Morehouse, Maggi M., and Zoe Trodd. *Civil War America: A Social and Cultural History*. New York, NY: Routledge, 2013.

Ruíz, Vicki, and Korrol, Virginia Sánchez. *Latina Legacies: Identity, Biography, and Community*. New York, NY: Oxford University Press, 2005.

Smith, Jon, and Deborah N. Cohn. *Look Away! The U.S. South in New World Studies*. Durham, NC: Duke University Press, 2004.

Velázquez, Loreta Janeta. *The Woman in Battle: A Narrative of the Exploits, Adventures, and Travels of Madame Loreta Janeta Velazquez*. Madison, WI: University of Wisconsin Press, 2003.

Wagenen, Michael Van. *Remembering the Forgotten War: The Enduring Legacies of the U.S./Mexican War*. Amherst, MA: University of Massachusetts Press, 2012.

INDEX

ABOUT THE AUTHOR

Ash Imery-Garcia was born in San Antonio, Texas. This is her second book for young adults about Latinos and Hispanics in the United States. She received her bachelor's degree in English literature from New York University, where she currently works full time.

PHOTO CREDITS